The Heyday of Swindon and its Locomotives

R. C. Riley

First published 1996

ISBN 0 7110 2482 0

Published by Ian Allan Publishing

an imprint of Ian Allan Ltd, Terminal House, Station Approach, Shepperton, Surrey TW17 8AS. Printed by Ian Allan Printing Ltd, Coombelands House, Coombelands Lane, Addlestone, Surrey KT15 1HY.

For Christine with thanks for her help and encouragement.

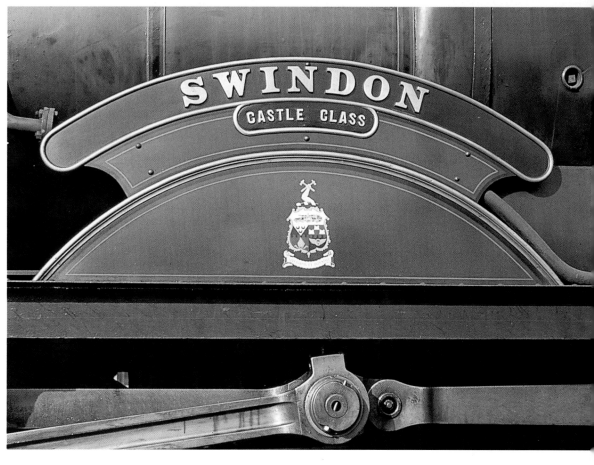

Front cover: 'Castle' class 4-6-0 No 5049 *Earl of Plymouth* in resplendent ex-works condition was being prepared for traffic at Swindon shed, 6 September 1959, having just been fitted with a double chimney.

Back cover: Swindon Works A Shop, 16 June 1957, with 'Hall' class 4-6-0 No 5911 *Preston Hall* nearing completion of an overhaul. At the bottom right can be seen the 8ft 0in driving wheels of broad gauge 4-2-2 *Lord of the Isles* built in 1851 and withdrawn in 1884. These are now in the GWR Museum.

Above: The 'Castle' class 4-6-0s were introduced in 1923 and, including 'Star' rebuilds, reached a total of 171 engines. The last to be built was named *Swindon* by HRH Princess Elizabeth on 15 November 1950. The nameplate on No 7037, with the Borough coat of arms, was recorded at Swindon on 18 March 1961.
R. C. Riley

Overleaf: Swindon locomotive shed, 1947.

All photos: R. C. Riley unless otherwise stated

Introduction

Isambard Kingdom Brunel's Great Western Railway reached Swindon from Paddington in 1840. In the following year the completed line to Bristol opened, as did the first part of the Cheltenham & Great Western Union Railway as far as Kemble. Less than 80 miles from London, this junction was deemed an ideal location for what was to become a very extensive railway works, established in 1843. Thus the history of Swindon was dramatically changed. A new town was set up near the station and Works and a 'railway village' was built to house workmen and their families; this mostly still survives, the buildings having been modernised internally and granted listed status. One remains in original condition and forms part of the GWR Museum. The other houses were taken over by the local authority in 1966. The Borough of Swindon was created in 1901 when Old and New Towns merged.

The GWR was fortunate in having some distinguished Locomotive Engineers. The first was 20-year-old Daniel Gooch, appointed in 1837 and already experienced in mechanical matters. He was responsible for construction of the Works and provision of motive power until his resignation in 1864. In the following year he was approached to become Chairman of the GWR, a post he held until his death in 1889. His successor was the greatly experienced Joseph Armstrong, the first to be given the title of Locomotive, Carriage & Wagon Superintendent. Under his supervision the Locomotive Works was further extended and in 1868 the decision was taken to build the Carriage & Wagon Works at Swindon. He was succeeded by William Dean in 1877 who held office for 25 years, a period which saw the end of the broad gauge. The halcyon years were those when G. J. Churchward was in charge, now termed Chief Mechanical Engineer, a time which saw the introduction of such locomotives as the 'Star' and 'Saint' class

4-6-0s, the powerful Class 28xx heavy freight engines, the first 2-8-0s in the country, and the versatile Class 43xx mixed traffic 2-6-0s.

Churchward also built the first British Pacific, *The Great Bear*, in 1908, its size and weight precluding it running anywhere other than between London and Bristol. It has been suggested that Churchward did not favour the engine and it was built at the suggestion of the Board for prestige reasons. However true this may be, it was rebuilt as a 'Castle' class 4-6-0 in 1924, three years after Churchward's retirement. C. B. Collett, his successor, followed a similar course. His 'Castle' class 4-6-0s were effectively modernised 'Stars' but the larger 'Kings' were a powerful new design, made possible only after the rebuilding of several underbridges to permit a greater axle load. Collett retired in 1941 and was succeeded by F. W. Hawksworth, who held office for eight years, by which time Nationalisation had taken place.

With each Mechanical Engineer, the Works was extended in size and character. The greatest extension was achieved in 1923 with the completion of the A Erecting Shop, the first part of which had been finished in 1900. Churchward was ahead of his time in many ways. He sent members of his team abroad, notably to the USA and France, to study locomotive development. From the latter country he purchased three compound Atlantics but trials showed conclusively that they did not have the edge on the products of Swindon. He introduced Belpaire fireboxes and superheating. The A Shop complex included a Locomotive Testing Plant. It is not surprising that other companies looked with envy at Swindon's products. However some criticism came from within; the 1908 Board of Trade returns showed expenditure on locomotive renewals and repairs to be the highest of any UK railway. Churchward was asked by the Board to justify why the LNWR could build three 4-6-0s for the cost of two of his design. Locomotive exchange trials took place, in which the 'Star' class 4-6-0s pitted against LNWR 'Experiment' class 4-6-0s, resulted in a one-sided contest totally vindicating Churchward's policies.

Let the last words on Churchward be those of Sir Nigel Gresley responding to Stanier's Presidential Address at the Institute of Locomotive Engineers in 1936:'I was pleased to hear Mr Stanier refer to his old chief, Mr Churchward, because I have always thought that locomotive engineers in this country owe more to the ingenuity, inventiveness and foresight of Churchward than to any other Chief Mechanical

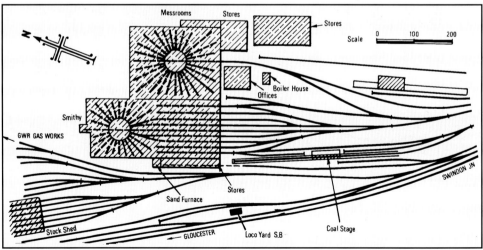

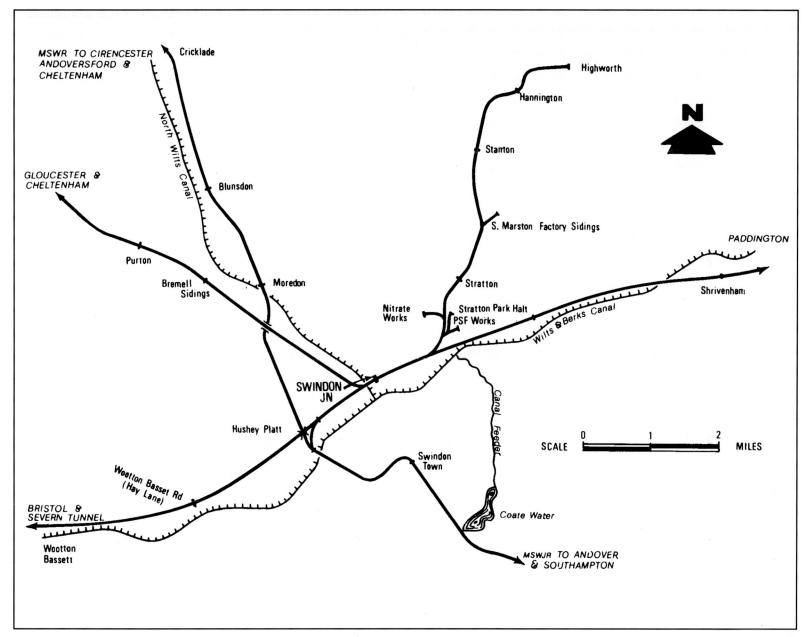

MSWR TO CIRENCESTER ANDOVERSFORD & CHELTENHAM

Cricklade

Highworth

Hannington

North Wilts Canal

Blunsdon

Stanton

GLOUCESTER & CHELTENHAM

S. Marston Factory Sidings

PADDINGTON

Purton

Bremell Sidings

Moredon

Stratton

Shrivenham

Nitrate Works

Stratton Park Halt
PSF Works

Wilts & Berks Canal

SWINDON JN

Canal Feeder

Rushey Platt

Swindon Town

SCALE

0   1   2

MILES

Wootton Basset Rd (Hay Lane)

Coate Water

BRISTOL & SEVERN TUNNEL

Wootton Bassett

MSWJR TO ANDOVER & SOUTHAMPTON

N

Engineer. I know that his influence on locomotives of this country still exists in a very marked way'.

In 1923 the final extension to the Iron Foundry was completed enabling high quality castings to be made for all railway and dock requirements. By that time, with a reliable supply of gas from its own gasworks and water pumped directly from the railway plant at Kemble, Swindon Works could be said to be virtually self-sufficient. Stores would be dispatched on a weekly rota basis to any station on the system by means of stores vans attached to stopping passenger trains. Two of these were particularly significant as they were clerestory roof bogie luggage vans from the 1897 Royal Train,

surviving as stores vans into BR days. The writer recalls one pause at a Cornish station, where the storeman produced a broom but would not issue it until satisfied that the bristles on the existing broom were sufficiently worn. In common with the other railway companies, the GWR had been compelled to introduce economies since the 1930s.

On the outbreak of war in 1939 Swindon Works rose to the occasion as it had done 25 years earlier. First assignment was preparation of over 100 'Dean Goods' 0-6-0s for service overseas. Then came manufacture of Hurricane fighter parts, heavy bombs and landing craft, to quote some examples. Wartime locomotive construction included further 'Hall' class 4-6-0s,

Class 28xx 2-8-0s and 0-6-PTs, together with 80 Stanier LMS Class 8F 2-8-0s. In 1947, the last year of the GWR, Swindon built 77 locomotives, 100 carriages and 1,707 wagons. It carried out heavy repairs on 777 locomotives, 2,722 carriages and 12,585 wagons, a reversion to normality after the war years. At this time the Works employed about 10,000 people, a figure soon to diminish.

Following Nationalisation the GWR proved reluctant to change its tried and tested ways. Notably it was unique in using Zeiss optical aligning equipment ensuring more accurate alignment of the frames and moving parts, thereby eliminating stresses. This led to a lengthening of the time in which the locomotive was in traffic between heavy repairs. Although BR established a testing plant at Rugby, the Swindon Plant saw increased use in conjunction with controlled road testing. In an early trial, a 19th century 'Dean Goods' 0-6-0 proved superior to a new LMR Ivatt Class 2MT 2-6-0, later modified as a result of lessons learnt. Among other locomotives tested were a Gresley Class V2 2-6-2 and the last BR express engine, No 71000 *Duke of Gloucester*.

However, the BR Modernisation Programme was instituted, emphasising that the future lay with diesel traction. This was to bring to an end steam at Swindon, and sadly led to closure of the Carriage Works in 1963, the entire Works suffering similarly in 1986.

Left: In steam days this was the station building at Swindon Junction, thus named to distinguish it from the former M&SWJR station at Swindon Town, which lost its passenger traffic in 1961. The 1842 down side building was recorded in July 1961. Local train services having been withdrawn, opportunity was taken to rationalise the layout, thus since 1968 all scheduled passenger services were diverted to use the former up platform, where the 1842 building remains. The down side building was demolished and station entry is now through the ground floor of a 12-storey office block. The old station illustrated was built of local sandstone. *T. Bryan*

Above: Rebuilt from 1923-built 'Star' class 4-6-0 No 4070 in 1939, 'Castle' class 4-6-0 No 5090 *Neath Abbey* enters Swindon on the 8.5am Weston-super-Mare to Paddington on Sunday, 26 April 1959, at the time of a change in carriage livery. This shows both down and up platforms. *Neath Abbey* survived in service for three more years. *R. C. Riley*

Left: Newly fitted with a double chimney, 'Castle' class 4-6-0 No 5066 *Sir Felix Pole* is released to traffic, having taken over the 9.15am Cheltenham–Paddington, 26 April 1959. This train was worked from Gloucester to Swindon by No 6985 *Parwick Hall.* No 5066, originally named *Wardour Castle*, acquired its new name in 1956 to commemorate a particularly successful General Manager, who held office from 1921 to 1929. *R. C. Riley*

Above: Ex-Works Class 42xx 2-8-0T No 5261 heads a down goods train past Swindon, 8 April 1964. This would have come from Swindon yard since it was virtually unknown for 2-8-0Ts to work east of Swindon. This was the second engine to carry this number; the first, built in 1926, was one of 40 relatively new engines placed in store due to the decline of the South Wales coal traffic. They were later rebuilt as Class 72xx 2-8-2Ts, the increased coal and water capacity enabling them to work main line freight trains in place of the elderly 'Aberdare' 2-6-0s. The last 14 rebuilds, Nos 7240–53, were randomly chosen from older stored members of the '42xx' class, which surprisingly in 1940 was augmented by the new engines, Nos 5255–64. *W. Potter*

Left: A pilot engine was always provided at the east end of Swindon, usually a small 2-6-2T, often a duty for an ex-Works engine. On 15 March 1958 it was Swindon-based '4575' class 2-6-2T No 5509, which would seem to have had a recent Works visit.
R. C. Riley

Above: On 26 April 1959 the pilot was again a Swindon-based engine, '8750' class 0-6-0PT No 9605, built in 1945. These engines had modified cabs compared with their largely similar Class 57xx predecessors. Between them they formed by far the largest GWR Class, 863 engines being built between 1929 and 1950. No 9605 was withdrawn in 1965 and the class became extinct the following year. *R. C. Riley*

Above: Leaving Swindon on 17 June 1962, 'Castle' class 4-6-0 No 5057 *Earl Waldegrave* was at the head of a Paddington–Cheltenham excursion. The miscellaneous carriage stock to be seen, ex-GWR, LNER and LMS respectively, suggests an ordinary excursion rather than a race special. The 'Earl' names carried by Nos 5043–62 were originally intended for the rebuilt 4-4-0s, Nos 3200–19, which were in later years known unofficially as the 'Dukedogs'. In fact Nos 3200–12 did actually carry these names for a few months — they were removed at the end of June 1937, the month in which the former Prime Minster, Stanley Baldwin, was ennobled,

the name *Earl Baldwin* being applied to No 5063. The '32xx' 4-4-0s were later renumbered in the '90xx' series. *W. Potter*

Right: Landore shed, Swansea, carried out the practice of applying silver paint to the buffer heads of its 'Castle' class 4-6-0s. On 6 September 1959, No 5077 *Fairey Battle* passes Swindon Works with the 9.55am Paddington–Swansea. This was one of 12 'Castles', Nos 5071–82, to lose the original names in 1940–41 and in a spirit of patriotism to take the names of aircraft then engaged in World War 2. *R. C. Riley*

Above: Stabled at Swindon when not in service was Track Testing Car No W139, converted from a 1911 Churchward 'Toplight' Brake Third. This was ingeniously fitted with whitewash apparatus worked by electrical impulse on encountering a bad stretch of track. It was also equipped with a Hallade track recorder, which maintained a continuous graph of all journeys. I encountered it in action as the rear vehicle in an up Worcester express at Slough West in 1963. Having photographed the train. I returned to the signalbox, then about to be closed — moments later the door was flung open and an irate ganger appeared to enquire whether we had identified the last coach. I told him it was the Track Testing Car. Muttering imprecations about the parentage of the engineers, the ganger complained that it was the second time in a fortnight that this had taken place and his gang had worked hard to rectify matters. With hindsight his visit was unnecessary; the whitewash was there for all to see. The coach survived in use until the mid-1980s, when it was added to the National Collection.
R. C. Riley

Left: Churchward's purpose-built Dynamometer Car of 1901 was in use for 60 years. It became very familiar in the 1950s when controlled road testing was carried out by Swindon Works, usually between Reading and Stoke Gifford. On one test in 1953, No 6001 *King Edward VII* had a load of 25 coaches including the Dynamometer Car, a tare weight of 796 tons. Such tests were not confined to WR engines. Recorded at Swindon Stock Shed in July 1964, Car W7W had been replaced three years earlier by a converted Hawksworth coach, latterly No DW 150192, which incorporated some of the equipment of the original coach. It survives in preservation. *R. C. Riley*

Above: By the 1960s Swindon was displaying signs of greater economy in its painting styles. Although the use of green paint continued on passenger classes, the practice of lining out was discontinued. On Swindon shed, 26 January 1964, Class 61xx 2-6-2T No 6141 gleamed in unlined green; it was to survive until the end of steam on WR lines in December 1965. Another repaint on the other side of the turntable was a good 'Modified Hall' often used on Worcester's 'Castle' duties, No 7928 *Wolf Hall*. It lasted until March 1965, by which time only four 'Castles' remained. *T. B. Owen*

Above: When asked to name their favourite engines the older enginemen frequently chose the two-cylinder 'Saint' class engines. Built between 1903 and 1913 they were very free-running engines and No 2915 *Saint Bartholomew* hauled the inaugural 'Cheltenham Flyer' express from Swindon to Paddington in July 1923. A total of 47 of the class survived to be included in BR stock. Of these, No 2934 *Butleigh Court* was recorded at Swindon, 11 June 1950, ex-Works in lined black livery; it survived for another two years. Many regretted the withdrawal of the last to remain in traffic, No 2920 *Saint David*, which was withdrawn in October 1953. *T. B. Owen*

Above: The first 'King' class 4-6-0 No 6000 *King George V* achieved fame soon after construction in 1927 when it was shipped to the USA to take part in the centenary celebrations of the Baltimore & Ohio Railroad; hence the presentation bell, suitably inscribed. Photographed on shed in September 1962, it was withdrawn three months later but was selected for preservation in the National Collection. Stored until 1968, it was loaned to Bulmer's cider makers of Hereford and overhauled by A. R. Adams & Co of Newport prior to exhibition. Following the end of steam in northwest England in 1968 BR had imposed a total steam ban. In November 1971 this was lifted to allow *King George V* to work a Bulmer's exhibition train to Birmingham, Kensington and Swindon. In 1972 steam-hauled special trains resumed on BR with Hereford-based No 6000 regularly appearing on the 'Welsh Marches Express' between Newport and Shrewsbury. When its main line certification ended, and with two other 'Kings' undergoing active overhaul, No 6000 was added to the collection of the GWR Museum at Swindon in 1992, replacing *Lode Star*, transferred to York. *J. G. Dewing*

Left: Between 1944 and 1950 Hawksworth built 71 'Modified Halls', improving the performance of the existing 'Halls', the first production engine having been built in 1928. 1944-built No 6967 *Willesley Hall*, on Swindon shed 16 June 1957, survived until the end of Western Region steam in December 1965. The 'Hall' class eventually numbered 330 engines.
R. C. Riley

Above: Hawksworth's other 4-6-0 design was the two-cylinder 'County' class, 30 powerful engines built between 1945 and 1947. No 1004 *County of Somerset* was standing outside Swindon shed on 16 June 1957. It had been fitted with a double chimney two months earlier, improving its performance if not enhancing its appearance. All were withdrawn by the end of 1964 and none have been preserved.
R. C. Riley

Above: Two ex-Works engines with different stories stand in the shed yard with the roof of the 1908 Roundhouse visible in the background on 16 June 1957. Class 28xx 2-8-0 No 3837, in a new coat of black paint, has just emerged from Swindon Works.

Class 43xx 2-6-0 No 4358 has been in traffic since overhaul at Caerphilly, once the works of the Rhymney Railway, rebuilt and extended by the GWR in 1926. Caerphilly had a distinctive trade mark, painting the reversing rod red. *R. C. Riley*

Above: On 6 September 1959, newly ex-Works Class 47xx 2-8-0 No 4703 stood in the shed yard. As with the mighty 'Kings', this handsome engine could be run in on a stopping passenger train to Didcot with perhaps only a two-coach B Set. Used mainly for overnight fitted freights, these mixed traffic 2-8-0s could be seen on expresses between Paddington and the West Country on summer Saturdays. Its gleaming appearance contrasts with that of the WD Austerity 2-8-0. Built in this form in 1922–3, the nine engines of this class were all withdrawn by May 1964.
R. C. Riley

Above: The running shed was situated alongside and to the east of the Gloucester line. It was opened in 1871 to replace a broad gauge shed alongside the Bristol line, the site of which was eventually used as an extension of the Works. Initially a nine-road shed, it later led into a roundhouse, while in 1908 another roundhouse was built alongside it to the east. The shed yard housed a distinguished visitor on 9 May 1964. It was Stanier's 4-6-2 No 46251 *City of Nottingham* which had worked through with a special for the RCTS from that city. Also evident are Nos 7022 *Hereford Castle* and 7929 *Wyke Hall,* incidentally the last of the class built. Stanier had spent 40 years at Swindon, latterly as Works Manager then assistant to the CME who was only five years older. It was for this reason that he accepted the post of CME on the LMS. *W. Potter*

Left: Outside the shed on the same date stood the oldest surviving restaurant car, No W9527W, built in 1906 for the Fishguard service. Its function at Swindon was to provide office accommodation, the roof of the 1871 building having been condemned as unsafe. The coach had been modernised in 1936 and placed on six-wheeled bogies three years later; it was later given Internal User No 079128. With the onset of dieselisation, Swindon shed closed in 1964. *R. C. Riley*

Below: The empty shed, 16 August 1964. In the distance was the roundhouse extension, the opening at right leading to the later roundhouse building. At Nationalisation in January 1948 Swindon had an allocation of 104 engines. *R. C. Riley*

Above: A group of Swindon-based engines keep company around the turntable, 12 November 1961. They consisted of '4575' class 2-6-2T No 5547, 0-6-0Ts Nos 3711, 6769 and 8783 of the '8750' class, and Class 22xx 0-6-0 No 2250. The '8750' 0-6-0PTs comprised those members of the '57xx' class built from 1933 onwards with modified cabs and other new features. The '67xx' series were fitted with steam brake only and three-link couplings purely for shunting work; Nos 6700–49 were built by contractors in 1930 and placed in store initially because of the recession. Following the withdrawal of older shunting engines 30 more were built, Nos 6750–79, in 1947–50. *T. B. Owen*

Right: In happier days engines stand around the turntable in the 1908 shed on 17 December 1961. Although by this time Swindon had 'Castles' on its allocation, none of the engines illustrated were Swindon based, a not unusual situation with some awaiting entry to works and others running in ex-Works. The Class 47xx 2-8-0 No 4706 was clearly in the latter category. *J. A. Coiley*

Left: Swindon would not be a place one would associate with heavy snowfalls. It is not known how often the services of Collett 0-6-0 No 2244, snowplough fitted, were required. It was recorded in Swindon shed on 26 January 1964. Withdrawal followed in 1965. One example, No 3205, survives in preservation on the West Somerset Railway. *W. Potter*

Above: Standing beside the coaling stage at Swindon, 26 May 1963, were 0-6-0PT No 3711, 4-6-0 No 4074 *Caldicot Castle* (second of the class to be built), 0-6-0PT No 4612 and 4-6-0 No 6933 *Birtles Hall*. No 3711 had been equipped to burn fuel oil by Robert Stephenson & Hawthorn in April 1958 and had undergone trials at Old Oak Common and Swindon. However, it was withdrawn in May 1963, as was No 4074, which had already lost its name and number plates. *W. Potter*

Above: Built in 1905, No 2810 was among the early members of Class 28xx 2-8-0s, incidentally the first examples of their wheel arrangement in the country. All were fitted with superheated boilers from 1909 and this became standard on new construction from 1911, commencing with No 2830. Clearly Aberdare shed thought well of No 2810 for it appears to have been cleaned for its last journey to Swindon as it stood in the Stock Shed yard, 20 September 1959, showing signs of a Caerphilly repaint. The Stock Shed was used to house engines temporarily surplus to requirements, but the future of those in the yard at this date was bleak. By 1959 pressure on the scrapyard was building up and the decision was taken to invite private tenders for the disposal of some WR engines in commercial scrapyards. No 2818 is preserved at the National Railway Museum. *W. Potter*

Right: The old 1842 gasworks in the Works complex having become inadequate for the extended Works' needs, a new gasworks was built to the north of the engine shed in 1874. With an initial ability to supply 250,000cu ft of gas per day, the plant was later extended when it was said to be the largest private gasworks in the world. It was finally closed in 1959, after which gas was supplied by the South Western Gas Board, which company took over one of the Works' gasholders. This closure provided more space as sidings for condemned locomotives, in this 14 August 1960 view, consisting of 0-6-0PTs, largely 10 years old or less. The first 10 of the '94xx' class were built at Swindon in 1947; the remaining 200 were contractor-built between 1949 and 1956. No 1652 in the foreground was one of 70 light 0-6-0PTs built to a restricted loading gauge, 1949-55, to replace the elderly '1901' class. *W. Potter*

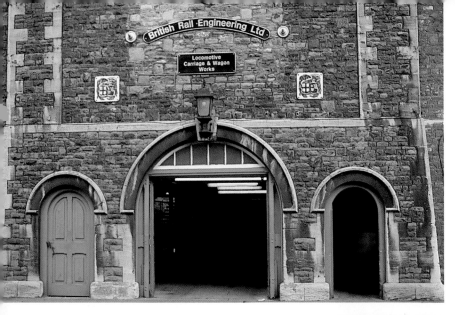

Left: With the continuing extension of the Works, notably in the 1864–77 period when Joseph Armstrong was Locomotive, Carriage & Wagon Engineer, it became necessary for safety reasons to build a new subway entrance from London Street, opened in February 1870. It was 300ft in length and 15ft wide but it had a restricted headroom of only 7ft. This 1984 view of what became known as the 'tunnel entrance' shows some additional ornamentation — even the GWR coats of arms were not original features. Here, every Wednesday at 2pm, other than in wartime, visitors were admitted for a guided tour of the Works, a practice started around the time of the opening of this entrance. A 1954 booklet quotes the admission fee as 6d (2.5p) or free if the return half of a ticket was shown! *R. C. Riley*

Right: The stone bas-reliefs above the entrance of the main office block were originally situated at either end of the 1841 broad gauge engine shed beside the main line to Bristol. With the threatened demolition of the building, about 1890, for proposed extension to the Works — this actually took place 40 years later — they were removed into safe custody. When it was decided to add a further storey to the office block in 1903 to provide a centralised drawing office, they were incorporated in the entrance wall in their later familiar position. The earliest broad gauge engines built by contractors to Brunel's specifications were miserable failures with two notable exceptions. Daniel Gooch took over as Locomotive Engineer in August 1837 before any of these engines had been delivered and he restored order to the unhappy situation. *R. C. Riley*

Above: The '1366' class 0-6-0PTs built in 1934 with a very short wheelbase replaced some obsolete Cornwall Minerals Railway engines. They were used on lines where there were sharp curves, notably Weymouth Harbour and Swansea Docks, while two were shedded at Swindon for use in the Wagon Works. No 1368 was recorded on the Works admission roads outside the offices on 1 March 1959. As their duties were taken over by diesels, their career took an unexpected turn. The three Beattie LSWR 2-4-0 well tanks of 1874–75 build had been the only engines found suitable to work from Wadebridge hauling trains of clay from Wenford Bridge. No 1368 was tried on the line in June 1962, found successful and then joined by Nos 1367 and 1369. They operated the branch until dieselisation at the end of 1964, when they were withdrawn. No 1369 survives in preservation on the South Devon Railway at Buckfastleigh, where it entered service in 1996. *W. Potter*

Above: The famous 4-4-0 No 3440 *City of Truro* emerged from Swindon in 1903, following appointment of G. J. Churchward as Locomotive, Carriage & Wagon Superintendent. Employed at Swindon since 1877, by 1896 he had been promoted to Works Manager, under William Dean, who in his last years relied heavily on Churchward. Thus, although the 'Cities' had the typical Dean double frames, the taper boiler and Belpaire firebox were Churchward features. *City of Truro's* claim to fame was that it attained an alleged 102.3mph down Wellington bank on 9 May 1904 on an Ocean Liner Mails special from Plymouth. On withdrawal in 1931 it went on display in the old York Railway Museum with its later number, 3717, green unlined livery and black frames. In 1957 it returned to Swindon, was overhauled and re-entered service, initially from Didcot, then at Swindon, where it was noted on an SLS Special, 25 August·1957, with its original number to avoid confusion with 0-6-0PT No 3717. The handsome livery was in the 1897 style.
R. C. Riley

Above: The '90xx' class double framed 4-4-0s, numbered in the '32xx' series until 1946, were introduced in 1936. They were intended for lines permitted only for engines with low axle loads, notably the former Cambrian Railways lines. They consisted of former 'Duke' class boilers, in some cases modernised, placed on the frames of withdrawn 'Bulldog' class 4-4-0s. Nos 3200-12 carried 'Earl' names originally but these were transferred to 'Castle' class 4-6-0s in 1937. With the strengthening of underbridges on secondary lines during the war they were gradually displaced by the lightweight 'Manor' class 4-6-0s or Class 43xx 2-6-0s. They were withdrawn between 1955 and 1960, the last survivor, No 9017, being privately preserved on the Bluebell Railway. Although built with cast iron chimneys as seen on No 9025 on its last visit to Swindon, 25 August 1957, most latterly carried copper cap chimneys. *R. C. Riley*

Left: Repainted engines in the Works yard, notably Hawksworth 'County' class 4-6-0 No 1002 *County of Berks*, 26 April 1959. Following trials on the Swindon Test Plant and on the road with No 1009 *County of Carmarthen* with a load of 22 coaches, it was decided to fit all engines of the class with a rather squat type of double chimney. No 1002 was so fitted in June 1958. Although the engine looks splendid in its middle chrome livery, Swindon tended to be a little economical with the varnish and the paint finish did not retain the brightness after a few weeks in service. In early BR days the 'Counties' were painted lined black but from May 1955, commencing with No 1020 *County of Monmouth*, they reverted to lined green livery, as carried by Nos 1000–29 when new in GWR days. *R. C. Riley*

Above: Swindon Works was involved in building BR Standard steam locomotives, as were most main works throughout the country. Swindon's share consisted of 80 Class 4MT 4-6-0s, 20 Class 3MT 2-6-0s, 45 Class 3MT 2-6-2Ts, ie the entire build in those cases, together with 34 Class 9F 2-10-0s. Only the express passenger 4-6-2s and 2-10-0 No 92220 were painted green; passenger and mixed-traffic engines were painted black lined out; freight engines black unlined. Swindon, having rediscovered green for its own engines, then proceeded to apply it to BR passenger and mixed traffic engines visiting the Works, hence the appearance of No 73054, a Bristol Barrow Road engine, outside the Works Foundry, 5 September 1959. *R. C. Riley*

Above: The 'Grange' class 4-6-0s, turned out from 1936, replaced withdrawn Class 43xx 2-6-0s, the frames and cylinders of which could be seen on the Dump awaiting scrap. These excellent mixed traffic engines, which used the wheels and motion from the engines they replaced, had a greatly improved front end design as compared with the 1928 design of the 'Halls'. They were well liked by the engine crews and it is sad that none survive in preservation. These engines were initially unlined black in BR days but lined green was introduced from 1956 — in prewar days they had been unlined green. As built they had 3,500gal tenders but as 4,000gal Collett tenders became available from withdrawn 'Stars' or new construction several 'Granges' were so fitted. None ran with a Hawksworth flush-sided type tender as seen to the left of No 6849 *Walton Grange* ex-Works, 15 March 1958.
R. C. Riley

Above: Hawksworth 'Modified Hall' class 4-6-0 No 6985 *Parwick Hall* stands outside the Reception Shop beside some coaled up but not repainted tenders, 6 September 1959. These tenders were effectively used as coal carriers for engines entering or emerging from works. At the left is the Works yard turntable and No 4920 *Dumbleton Hall* now preserved. In the distance, also illustrated in the previous picture, can be seen the Pattern Store surmounted by a large water tank of 225,000gal capacity. This building still remains. There being insufficient water locally to supply the Works' needs, water was pumped down from Kemble, 13 miles away, an arrangement completed in 1903. Several 'Halls' and 'Modified Halls' survive in preservation. *R. C. Riley*

Above: Churchward's choice for general purpose mixed traffic work was the Class 43xx 2-6-0s, of which 322 were built between 1911 and 1925. A further 20 heavier 2-6-0s entered service in 1932, originally Nos 9300–19. From 1956 their total weight was reduced by $1^1/_2$ tons giving them greater route availability and they were renumbered 7322–41 to follow on from the existing series. No 7338 was recorded on 15 March 1958. One of each type is preserved: No 5322 at the Didcot Railway Centre and No 7325 on the Severn Valley Railway.
R. C. Riley

Above: Heading a row of engines outside A Shop on 16 August 1964 was 'Manor' class 4-6-0 No 7803 *Barcote Manor*. These 30 engines were a lightweight version of the 'Granges' with shorter frames and smaller boilers, thereby increasing their route availability. From September 1963 the once familiar 89C shed code of Machynlleth was altered to 6F in the LMR Chester Division. With the ongoing withdrawal of GWR engines superseded by diesel traction, the Works was accepting LMR 2-6-0s for overhaul, hence the appearance of No 43137 and another of its type. The Great Western Society acquired No 7808 *Cookham Manor* from BR but a further eight can be found on preserved railways having been rescued from Woodham's Barry scrapyard. With the onset of BR, 'Manors' were painted in unlined black with the exception of Nos 7820–9 built at Swindon in 1950 in lined black livery. On overhaul they reverted to unlined black but from 1956 lined green livery was introduced. Like the 'Granges', they were unlined in prewar days.
R. C. Riley

Left: With its modern chimney and small safety valve bonnet No 4062 *Malmesbury Abbey* looked a modern engine until the small cab without a side window was noted, while the elbow type outside steam pipe was a unique feature of those members of the 'Star' class so fitted. Following introduction of *North Star* in 1906, 60 more 'Stars' were built between 1907 and 1914. The final series, Nos 4061–72 named after abbeys, were built in 1922–23. Five of the earlier engines were rebuilt to 'Castles' in the mid-1920s, and the last 10 'Abbeys' followed in the late 1930s. No 4062 was recorded outside A Shop on 27 April 1952, being withdrawn nearly five years later. *T. B. Owen*

Above: No 4082 *Windsor Castle*, newly built, was driven from the Works to the Station by His Majesty King George V on the occasion of a royal visit to Swindon in April 1924, brass plates being affixed to the cabside to commemorate the occasion. When HM King George VI died in February 1952, No 4082 was a high mileage engine stopped at Worcester awaiting overhaul. The WR gave instructions for its plates to be transferred to postwar-built 'Castle' No 7013 *Bristol Castle*, which engine differed in several details from No 4082. A photograph of the royal funeral train was reproduced in *The Times* and an eagle-eyed reader wrote to the letters column protesting that the engine was not *Windsor Castle* and was not entitled to carry the brass plates commemorating HM King George V's visit. Having been so publicly criticised, the WR removed the brass plates but the two engines never regained their correct identities. No 4082 *Windsor Castle* recorded at Swindon, 22 April 1963, was really the 1948-built No 7013. Remarkably the 1924 engine survived until 1965, outliving its successor by several months. *J. P. Mullett*

Above: One of the more famous members of the class, 4-6-0 No 4079 *Pendennis Castle* was standing outside A Shop, 11 April 1965, following overhaul, having been privately preserved. First of the class, No 4073 *Caerphilly Castle* was exhibited at the British Empire Exhibition, Wembley in 1924 bearing a notice that it was 'the most powerful passenger locomotive in the British Isles'. This did not find favour with the LNER contingent whose new 4-6-2 *Flying Scotsman* was also on display. It is said that at the behest of the LNER trials took place between examples of each type on the

East Coast main line from King's Cross to Doncaster and on the GWR from Paddington to Plymouth and back. *Pendennis Castle* was the engine used on the ECML and the general outcome greatly favoured the GWR engine resulting in improvements to the Gresley Pacific design. As a result, this was the GWR representative at the Wembley Exhibition in 1925. Its later history was unexpected — it was sold to Hammersley Iron Pty Ltd in Western Australia in 1977, where it still remains. *W. Potter*

Above: Looking somewhat woebegone, 4-6-0 No 6018 *King Henry VI* made a late appearance in the Works yard, 26 May 1963. Officially condemned in December 1962 it made a purposeful run with a 410-ton load from Birmingham to Swindon and back with a Stephenson Locomotive Society Special on 28 April 1963, hence the inappropriate Tyseley shed code. Speed reached the eighties more than once, with a brief flurry at 90mph, not bad for an engine about to be scrapped. It has been suggested that Butlin's expressed an interest in it for display at one of their holiday camps. However, the price asked by the WR was regarded as excessive and another LMR 'Duchess' was purchased instead. A similar story concerns the LNER Pacific *Silver Link*. In 35 years' service No 6018 attained a mileage of 1,738,387; some 200,000 miles less than No 6013, the highest mileage 'King'.
W. Potter

Above: Standing outside A Shop, 18 September 1955, were three ex-Works engines. Class 43xx 2-6-0 No 5380 has had a general overhaul and a black repaint. The two 'Hall' class 4-6-0s have been 'soled and heeled', ie they have had intermediate repairs with repainted smokebox, chimney and front buffer beam, at that time still in the lined black livery. The engines concerned were No 5988 *Bostock Hall* and No 4912 *Berrington Hall*.
R. C. Riley

Above: Four years later, 6 September 1959, another group of engines newly out of shops stand in the Works yard. By this time lined green had been introduced. This group consists of Class 43xx 2-6-0 No 5385, Class 61xx 2-6-2T No 6103 and 'Hall' class 4-6-0 No 6985 *Parwick Hall*. Note again that the tank engine has had only an intermediate repair, just the smokebox, chimney and buffer beam having had the painters' attention, indicating that the boiler has not been removed from the frames.
R. C. Riley

Left: No 2008, an 0-6-0PT of the '1901' class built at Wolverhampton Works in 1892 as a saddle tank and modified with pannier tanks 30 years later. Despite their modest size they were strong little engines and their light weight and short wheelbase made them ideal for dock shunting work. A total of 43 of these engines survived to enter BR stock, two of which, Nos 1925 and 2007, remained in saddle tank form. No 2008 from Birkenhead shed was the penultimate survivor, having just been withdrawn when seen at Swindon on 15 March 1958. Like many of the older 0-6-0PTs it still retained an open cab. *R. C. Riley*

Above: A later and slightly larger type of Wolverhampton-built six-coupled tank was the '2021' class, of which an example was No 2070 at Swindon, 18 September 1955, on its last journey to the scrapyard. Remarkably several engines of this type, even from sheds as far away as Cornwall or West Wales, were overhauled at Crewe or Derby Works between 1948 and 1951. No 2127 of Taunton emerged from Crewe early in 1949 with its number plate having a red background in true LNWR style. This practice was extended in an inconsistent way to any ex-GWR engines overhauled from the spring of 1950. It did not go well on green engines and an edict of 1952 stated that 'the practice was to be discontinued due to objections by the public!' No 2070 illustrates this but still retained the letters GWR on the tank sides. In the background outside A Shop there was another view of No 5380 gleaming in a new coat of black paint. *R. C. Riley*

Above: The first 30 of the 45xx 2-6-2Ts were built at Wolverhampton. All later engines and those of the '4575' class were built at Swindon. No 4507 of Yeovil was awaiting repair at Swindon, 6 September 1959. On withdrawal four years later it was the last surviving engine built at Wolverhampton. These small engines with 4ft 7½in driving wheels had a remarkable turn of speed on branch lines where permissible and on main line stopping trains. Some of the later engines of both types survive in preservation. *R. C. Riley*

Right: The aristocrats of the 2-6-2T classes were the 70 Class 61xx engines built for London area accelerated services between 1931 and 1935. They became displaced and saw more widespread use with the introduction of DMUs from 1960. Nevertheless, No 6167 seen on 26 May 1963 still carried the Slough shed code, but the class was to become extinct in 1965. No 6106 survives at the Didcot Railway Centre. The engine was standing outside the Weighbridge House, where all locomotives were weighed when ex-Works. It was announced in 1995 that this building was to be taken over by the locally based Archer's Brewery. This has led to a labour intensive effort by members of the Friends of Swindon Railway Museum to recover all equipment for eventual display. *W. Potter*

Left: Newly released into the Works yard by means of the traverser in A Shop, Class 42xx 2-8-0T No 4272 was stabled on 6 November 1960. Introduced in 1910 and intended primarily for short-haul coal and steel traffic, 195 engines of the class had been built by 1930. Because of the trade recession, Nos 5275–94 never entered traffic and Nos 5255–74 spent most of their lives in store. Between 1934 and 1936 these 40 engines were rebuilt to 2-8-2Ts suitable for main line work with increased water capacity and coal capacity doubled. In 1940 a further 10 2-8-0Ts were built, Nos 5255–64. They were not commonly seen at Swindon, overhauls usually being carried out at Caerphilly. *R. C. Riley*

Above: Outside the Weighbridge House is Class 72xx 2-8-2T No 7240, the first of 14 of the older Class 42xx 2-8-0Ts to be rebuilt in 1937, formerly No 4239, and chosen from engines of the class still in store. These engines were familiar in the London area and the Midlands, notably on coal trains from South Wales but also on general freight traffic. They were intended to replace the ageing 'Aberdare' 2-6-0s in course of withdrawal. *W. Potter*

Left: An engine with an unusual history was seen outside A Shop on 20 September 1964. A member of the Taff Vale Railway Class 01 0-6-2Ts, TVR No 28, it became GWR No 450 after the 1923 Grouping. It was built at the TVR Cardiff West Yard Works in 1897, being withdrawn in 1926 and placed on the Sales List. The following year it was bought by the Woolmer Instructional Military Railway, where it bore the name *Gordon*. At the same time a Class M 0-6-2T, GWR 579 (TVR No 168), built by Kitson & Co in 1886, was purchased and given the name *Kitchener*. The WIMR became known as the Longmoor Military Railway in 1935 and the older 0-6-2T was scrapped five years later. During World War 2 *Gordon* became WD No 205 (later 70205), being withdrawn at the end of 1947 and sold to James N. Connell, Coatbridge for the South Hetton Colliery. It was finally withdrawn in 1960 by which time the many 0-6-2Ts from the absorbed railways in South Wales had been withdrawn by BR. After lengthy negotiations the NCB presented this engine to the British Transport Commission for preservation as a representative of the once familiar type of engine most prominent in the South Wales valleys. *R. C. Riley*

Above: After storage in many locations, the one time *Gordon* was moved to the Harold Wilson Industrial Estate, Caerphilly, which prior to closure in 1964, was better known as the GWR Caerphilly Works, substantially rebuilt in 1926 from that of the Rhymney Railway. Here the engine was restored by members of the Caerphilly Railway Society. As a former Longmoor trainee, the writer travelled to Wales on 22 June 1991 to see TVR No 28 on display. Another TVR 0-6-2T, Class 02 No 426 (TVR No 85) was sold in 1929 to the Lambton, Hetton & Joicey Colliery in Durham. It was acquired by the Keighley & Worth Valley Railway in 1970 and is currently being restored to its original condition. Later built 0-6-2Ts from the South Wales companies were mostly 'Great Westernised' with standard boilers, while older engines were replaced by 200 Class 56xx 0-6-2Ts built between 1924 and 1928. One of these, No 6697, survives at the Didcot Railway Centre and TVR No 28 is undergoing overhaul on the Dean Forest Railway. *R. C. Riley*

Above: Probably the most successful of the BR Standard steam designs was the Class 9F 2-10-0, of which 251 were built between 1954 and 1960. First of the class, No 92000, outside A Shop, was repainted on 18 March 1960, the day on which the last BR steam engine was named inside the erecting shop. No 92000 was built with a single chimney but the WR fitted Nos 92000–2/5/6 with double chimneys as a result of Controlled Road Testing. New constructions from No 92183 upwards were also fitted. The engines chosen to work summer extra passenger trains over the Somerset & Dorset line were selected from the double chimney batch. Note the comparison with the Class 28xx 2-8-0.
J. A. Coiley

THE LAST STEAM LOCOMOTIVE TO BE BUILT BY BRITISH RAILWAYS

"EVENING STAR"

BUILT IN SWINDON WORKS AND NAMED ON MARCH 18TH 1960

92220

Above: Destined to have a very short lifespan in BR ownership, the last of 999 BR Standard steam engines to be built was Class 9F 2-10-0 No 92220 *Evening Star*, ceremonially named in A Shop, 18 March 1960, by K. W. C. Grand, Member of the British Transport Commission. Unlike the remaining Class 9F 2-10-0s, it was painted lined green and fitted with a copper-capped chimney. Initially allocated to Cardiff Canton, it attained a degree of fame when it worked the up 'Red Dragon' to Paddington on three consecutive days in the summer of 1960. This practice was stopped by higher authority because the sight of a supposedly heavy freight engine maintaining express train schedules focused attention on the unenterprising timings of such prestige services. *Evening Star* spent two summers on the Somerset & Dorset Joint Line, in 1962–63, and in the former it worked the last Up and Down 'Pines Express' over that route. It was withdrawn in 1965 for preservation, eventually for display at the National Railway Museum, York. It has subsequently proved a popular choice for main line steam specials. Built in the years of steam's decline, many Class 9F 2-10-0s had equally short lives despite their undoubtedly successful design. *J. A. Coiley*

Above: The displayed highlight in the A Erecting Shop was the *North Star* replica built in 1925 for the railway centenary celebrations. This engine and *Morning Star* bought from R. Stephenson & Co were the first successful GWR engines. Ten similar engines were ordered by Daniel Gooch, with some future orders being based on these designs, so introducing an element of standardisation at an early date. In fact *North Star* hauled the Director's train to Maidenhead in May 1838, prior to formal public opening. *North Star* survived in traffic in rebuilt form until 1871 and was then preserved at Swindon Works with the 4-2-2 *Lord of the Isles*; both were scrapped in 1906 because of space problems, a decision later regretted. When the replica *North Star* was built it was said to be remarkable how many parts of the original were found! This engine is preserved in the GWR Museum, Swindon. *R. C. Riley*

Right: The 6ft 8¹/₂in driving wheels in the foreground were those of No 3440 *City of Truro*, receiving major attention on 4 March 1962 prior to entry to the GWR Museum, where it was to spend the next 23 years. At right was No 6012 *King Edward VI* in Swindon Works for the last time and undergoing a light repair; it was withdrawn six months later. *T. B. Owen*

Above: Interior of A Shop, 3 May 1959, with six ex-GWR and two BR engines receiving attention. Of note is the new double chimney just fitted to No 1029 *County of Worcester*. More distant, No 6029 *King Edward VIII* had already received a double chimney in December 1957, alteration of 'Kings' to this form being completed a year later.

T. B. Owen

Above: With less than two years to go for Western Region steam, engines were still being overhauled on 26 January 1964. Class 56xx 0-6-2T No 5691 would normally have been overhauled at Caerphilly Works, which closed in 1963, and had been repainted black; a few years earlier it would have expected to bear lined green livery. Also to be seen were Nos 6859 *Yiewsley Grange* and 6816 *Frankton Grange*, both to survive until the second half of 1965. The live wires were for operation of the traverser.
W. Potter

Above: Loaded on to a trolley a new 'King' class double chimney awaits fitting to the next engine due for conversion, 16 June 1957. This alteration to the 'Kings' was carried out between September 1955 and December 1958. A similar change was made to 66 of the 'Castle' class 4-6-0s between May 1956 and December 1961. *R. C. Riley*

Right: A variety of wheels recorded outside A Shop on 4 May 1958. No trace remains of this once modern and well-equipped erecting shop, which was totally demolished after closure of the Works. *T. B. Owen*

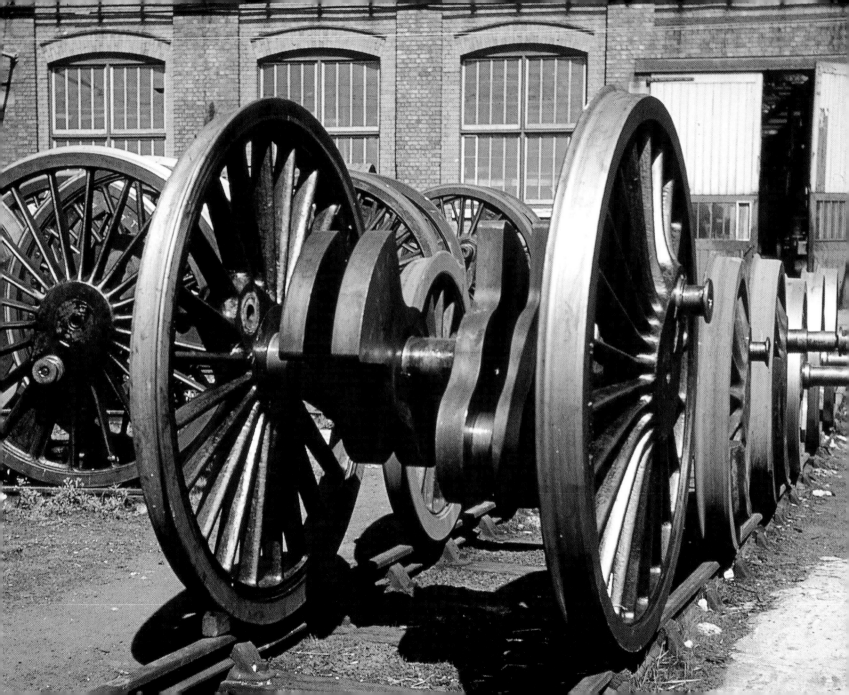

Above: It will have been noted that engines were separated from their tenders in the Works yard before entering the erecting shops. Tenders were overhauled in part of B Shop and here a group of mainly repainted tenders were recorded on 16 February 1958. The nearest tender, clearly not from a GWR engine, was that of a BR Standard Class 2MT 2-6-0 embellished by Swindon in lined green livery. *W. Potter*

Left: The Central Boiler Station at Swindon Works in 1939 had eight chimneys, each consisting of six boiler barrels said to be from 'Dean Goods' 0-6-0s. Truly it was an example of 'waste not, want not!' By 14 October 1962 the Works' output had been reduced as had the height of the chimneys, only 25 boiler barrels being identifiable. *T. B. Owen*

Above: Locomotive preservationists eat your heart out! By virtue of their position in the Concentration Yard near C Shop it is certainly a one-way journey for these boilers, some of which had been overhauled, seen on 24 March 1963. In the distance the impressive size of the A Erecting Shop can be observed. Finished in 1921, it covered an area of 502,975sq ft, now just a memory. *T. B. Owen*

Right: Another tidy line-up of boilers in the boiler park in May 1964. With the end of WR steam just over 18 months away it was unlikely that they would see further use. *R. Hobbs*

Above: At the end of September 1960 'Grange' class 4-6-0 No 6801 *Aylburton Grange* was seen laid aside on Penzance shed in the usual immaculate condition of that shed's engines. It had been given the shed's last respects, having been cleaned to go to Swindon for scrap, the first of the class to be withdrawn. On Swindon Works Dump, 5 November 1960, the external polish has worn off but No 6801 still looks in good condition. Apart from a few months in its early days it had spent its life in the West Country, mostly at Penzance. They were deservedly popular engines and by January 1964 there were still 74 in service of 80 engines built. By the end of WR steam in December 1965, the last of them were withdrawn and none survive. *R. C. Riley*

Right: C Shop in the background was used for cutting up engines but by the late 1950s the number requiring attention meant that many had to be dealt with in the open. On 15 March 1958 the torch starts its deadly work on Class 54xx 0-6-0PT No 5419, one of 25 engines built 1931–2 for pull and push working. There were 40 similar engines of the '64xx' class with smaller driving wheels. Branch line closures and dieselisation brought about their demise. *R. C. Riley*

Above: The scale of the steam withdrawal programme had been appreciated by the WR, which had started sending condemned engines to private scrapyards in March 1959. Nevertheless, a considerable amount of cutting up was done at Swindon and extra sidings were provided to house those engines waiting attention. The 'Castle' on the Dump still retaining name and number plates was unusual by this time, 15 April 1962. Ten modernised 0-6-0PTs had been built at Swindon in 1947, Nos 9400–9. On the eve of Nationalisation the GWR announced that it had ordered 200 more from contractors. Delivery of these was slow and eventually spread from 1949 to 1956 and the class had very short lives. No 9474, seen here, entered service in 1955 and lasted only 6½ years; a later example, No 9499, had a life in traffic of just over four years. *T. B. Owen*

Right: Only a fortnight later and some shunting has taken place; the 'Castle' is identified as No 5004 *Llanstephan Castle*, while another 'Castle' with nameplates can be seen. The 'Mogul' has lost its safety valve cover. The size of A Shop is again apparent. Alongside the main line to Bristol many covered wagons await their fate. It was due to the fact that Woodham's Barry scrapyard gave priority to breaking up non-passenger rolling stock that so many steam locomotives escaped the cutter's torch. *J. A. Coiley*

Above: The Works having been established on a greenfield site, the need was soon established for a large lodging house, opened in 1849. By the 1860s adequate housing was available and the building became a Wesleyan Chapel in 1869, remaining so for some 90 years. On 22 June 1962, the next phase of its life began as the GWR Museum. The large exhibits entered the museum at weekends during April and May. First in was 'Dean Goods' 0-6-0 No 2516, of which 160 were built between 1883 and 1889. They served overseas in the two world wars. In 1914–18, 62 saw service, of which eight failed to return. In 1939–40 a further 108 were sold to the War Department, of which 79 were lost in France after German occupation. In the immediate postwar years a number of these rediscovered engines were sent to China, truly a much travelled class.

T. E. Williams

Above: The famed *City of Truro*, which had re-entered traffic between 1957 and 1961, was restored to its 1920 condition and regained its latter-day number, 3717, before entering the museum. It retained this austere livery until 1985 when it emerged from the museum as part of the Great Western's 150th anniversary celebrations. It regained the number 3440 and the elaborate 1897 livery following overhaul at Bridgnorth on the Severn Valley Railway, on which line it ran for some months. Its similar forays in 1985–91 included main line trips, loans to preserved railways and the undoubted highlight was to represent British steam at the Netherlands Railways' 150th anniversary celebrations at Utrecht. It reappeared at Swindon for the 'National Railway Museum on Tour' event in 1990 and after further preserved railway visits was in steam for the reopening of the Great Hall of the National Railway Museum in April 1992, remaining there to this day. *T. B. Owen*

Above: The 0-6-0 pannier tank design was a distinctive GWR feature, first introduced on an experimental engine in 1898. Soon afterwards the decision was taken to introduce pannier tanks, since the new use of Belpaire fireboxes did not facilitate saddle tank construction. It was not until 1910 that the changeover started with the conversion of existing engines and, with the exception of the '1361' class dock tanks, no new engines were built in saddle tank form. When selection of engines for the museum was considered the choice went to the last pre-Nationalisation design, the '94xx' class 0-6-0PT. No 9400 was recorded during its move into the museum on 9 April 1962. As evidence of the standardisation instituted in the Churchward era, the Standard No 10 boiler on No 9400 was of a type introduced in 1924 to modernise the former Taff Vale Railway 0-6-2Ts and some of those of the Rhymney Railway and Brecon & Merthyr Railway. The boiler now fitted to No 9400 was first fitted to ex-M&SWJR 4-4-2T No 27 in 1924 and later to an ex-M&SWJR 0-6-0. This type of boiler was also fitted to Collett's Class 22xx 0-6-0s. *T. E. Williams*

Above: First choice to represent GWR express passenger design was Churchward 4-6-0 No 4003 *Lode Star*, built in 1907. The four-cylinder 'Stars' and two-cylinder 'Saints' shared the express work until the introduction in 1923 of the 'Castle' class designed by C. B. Collett following Churchward's retirement. A total of 47 'Star' class 4-6-0s survived into BR ownership, together with a further 15 which had been rebuilt as 'Castles'. The 'Star' names were taken from the earliest broad gauge engines of 1837–41. Last of the class to be withdrawn was No 4056 *Princess Margaret* in October 1957. In 1992 *Lode Star* was transferred to the NRM at York, its place being taken by No 6000 *King George V*. The museum is set to expand with its proposed move into No 20 Shop, formerly R Shop in the Works complex. *T. B. Owen*

Above: One of the many coal trains from South Wales approaches Wootton Bassett, 18 September 1955, in charge of modified Class 28xx 2-8-0 No 3846. In the following year the Clean Air Act was passed with the introduction of smokeless zones and hence led to a reduction in such traffic. West of the station the junction off the Bristol main line forming the South Wales Direct line was opened in 1903. Prior to this Welsh traffic had proceeded via Gloucester. At the time this photograph was taken from the Junction signalbox, Wootton Bassett station originated some milk tank traffic but the station was closed in 1965. *R. C. Riley*

Above: Repainted in green unlined livery, Swindon-based Class 43xx 2-6-0 No 6320 shunts an engineer's spent ballast train at Dauntsey, 6 November 1960. Unusually by this date, the engine was not fitted with outside admission steam pipes to the cylinders. No 6320 was the only member of its class to be fitted for oil burning in the abortive scheme of 1947–49. Until 1951 Dauntsey was the junction for trains to Malmesbury. *R. C. Riley*

Left: On a Swindon Works running in turn, Class 47xx 2-8-0 No 4705 pauses at Challow with the 10.25am Didcot to Swindon on 13 May 1961. In the distance is the large Brunel two-road goods shed. Challow, originally Faringdon Road, served Wantage and Faringdon when it first opened, hence the large broad gauge goods shed. *R. C. Riley*

Above: Much of the line between Swindon and Didcot was double track only with passing loops at several stations. Uffington, junction for the branch to Faringdon, did not have this facility. 'Hall' class 4-6-0 No 6957 *Norcliffe Hall* was seen at the head of an up parcels train approaching the station on Sunday, 26 April 1959. *R. C. Riley*

Above: The Highworth branch, just over 5½ miles in length, was an impecunious local line, construction of which began in 1878. The company soon ran into difficulties and sold out to the GWR in 1882, with opening taking place the following year. Since a number of Works employees lived by this line, a return workmen's train was run for their benefit from 1890. As a loss-making branch it closed in February 1953, the last train being hauled by non-auto fitted Class 58xx 0-4-2T No 5800, a class associated with the line since entry into traffic in 1933. The workmen's train continued to run until August 1962, by which time the track was in poor condition. Having enjoyed free travel, the workmen had to pay their fares on the replacement buses! Class 16xx 0-6-0T No 1658 was recorded at Highworth on a Railway Club brake van special, 13 May 1961. *R. C. Riley*

Right: Unlike the Highworth branch, the 3½-mile line from Uffington to Faringdon was a broad gauge line opened in June 1864 and converted to standard gauge in 1878. Such a short line could never be a paying proposition in the motor era and the passenger service was withdrawn at the end of 1951. In the 1950s railway societies could charter special trains over closed branches and request specific motive power. Such was the case with this Railway Enthusiasts' Club special in charge of '1361' class 0-6-0ST No 1365 on 26 April 1959. The five engines of this class spent most of their lives at Plymouth for shunting in Millbay Docks. No 1365 had been transferred to Swindon by 1957. Finally allocated to Bristol St Philip's Marsh, it was withdrawn in 1962. No 1363 survives in preservation at the Didcot Railway Centre. *R. C. Riley*

Above: To the dismay of the GWR, another railway company had the audacity to serve Swindon. Formed by the amalgamation of two local lines, the Swindon, Marlborough & Andover Railway and the Swindon & Cheltenham Extension Railway, the resultant Midland & South Western Junction Railway became a cross-country line, less busy than but having some similarities to the more famous Somerset & Dorset Joint Railway. It connected Cheltenham with Andover and thence by running powers to Southampton. Its line crossed the Bristol main line at Rushey Platt, very close to the Works C Shop. The M&SWJR was absorbed by the GWR at the Grouping of 1923. The M&SWJR had its works at Cirencester and its Head Office at Swindon Old Town station, where *City of Truro* was recorded on a southbound special train, 14 May 1960. The former M&SWJR offices can be seen to the left of the tree above the rear of the train. All passenger services were withdrawn in 1961. *W. Potter*

Above: The Wantage Tramway was a purely local line, 2½ miles in length, linking the market town with the GWR station at Wantage Road, opened to horse traction in 1875 and steam traction a year later. Initially, use was made of steam tram engines, appropriate to roadside use, but in 1878 a four-coupled well tank built by George England & Co in 1857 for the short-lived Sandy & Potton Railway, was purchased from its subsequent owners, the LNWR. As Wantage Tramway Co No 5 it was the mainstay of the line until 1893 when a five-year-old 'Manning Wardle' 0-4-0ST was acquired, WTC No 7. In 1925 the GWR introduced a road motor service covering the route and the Wantage directors came to agreement with the GWR that the latter company should take over the passenger and parcels traffic. Nevertheless, both engines continued to maintain the freight service for a further 20 years. They had been overhauled at Swindon Works from time to time and at the sale of plant the GWR successfully bid £100 for No 5. Following attention at Swindon, when it regained its original name *Shannon*, it was placed on display at Wantage Road until that station closed in 1964. It was recorded there on 26 April 1959. It is now at the Didcot Railway Centre. *R. C. Riley*

Railway Classics from IAN ALLAN Publishing

The Heyday of Leeds Holbeck & its Locomotives
By Gavin Morrison ISBN: 0711022259 7.5in x 9.5in H/B **£10.99**

The Heyday of Steam Around Manchester
By Tom Heavyside ISBN: 0711023298 7.5in x 9.5in H/B **£10.99**

The Heyday of the DMU
By Alan C. Butcher ISBN: 0711023190 7.5in x 9.5in H/B **£10.99**

The Heyday of Nine Elms & its Locomotives
By Colin Boocock ISBN: 0711020671 7.5in x 9.5in H/B **£9.95**

On London & South Western Lines
By Alan C. Butcher ISBN: 071102331X 7.5in x 9.5in H/B **£10.99**

On London & North Western Lines
By Derek Huntriss ISBN: 0711023824
7.5in x 9.5in H/B **£10.99**

On Great Central Lines
By Robert Robotham ISBN: 0711022445 7.5in x 9.5in H/B **£10.99**

On Cambrian Lines
By Derek Huntriss ISBN: 0711021856 7.5in x 9.5in H/B **£10.99**

On Great Northern Lines
By Derek Huntriss ISBN: 0711022860
7.5in x 9.5in H/B **£10.99**

On Somerset &Dorset Lines
By Robert Robotham ISBN: 0711024138
7.5in x 9.5in H/B **£10.99**

On the Waverley Route
By Robert Robotham ISBN: 0711024146 7.5in x 9.5in H/B **£10.99**

HOW TO ORDER: Simply call **IAN ALLAN MAIL ORDER DEPT ON 01903 732596**, quoting reference code **HSR01**, your credit card details and the ISBN of the book(s) required. Alternatively, write to: **Littlehampton Book Services, Dept HSR01, 10-14 Eldon Way, Lineside Estate, Littlehampton, West Sussex BN17 7HE.** Fax: 01903 730914. **(Please add £2.50 post and packing charges).**

For further information on Ian Allan Publishing/Dial House titles, or for a copy of our Books and Videos Catalogue, contact: The Marketing Department on **01932 855909**.